Read & Respond

FOR KS1

Read & Respond

Illustrations. Axel Scheffler and Anna Godwin, Beehive Illustration.

Text © 2010 Sara Stanley © 2010 Scholastic Ltd

Designed using Adobe InDesign

Published by Scholastic Ltd,
Book End, Range Road, Witney,
Oxfordshire OX29 0YD
www.scholastic.co.uk

Printed by Bell & Bain
1 2 3 4 5 6 7 8 9   6 7 8 9 0 1 2 3 4 5

British Library Cataloguing-in-Publication Data
A catalogue record for this book is available from
the British Library.
ISBN 978-1407-11864-2

The rights of Sara Stanley to be identified as the the author of this work has been asserted by her in accordance with the Copyright, Designs and Patents Act 1988.

Extracts from the Primary National Strategy's Primary Framework for Literacy (2006) nationalstrategies.standards.dcsf.gov.uk/primary/primaryframework/literacyframework © Crown copyright. Reproduced under the terms of the Click Use Licence.

Acknowledgements

The publishers gratefully acknowledge permission to reproduce the following copyright material: **Scholastic Ltd** for the use of extracts and illustrations from *Stick Man* by Julia Donaldson and illustrated by Axel Scheffler. Text © 2008, Julia Donaldson, illustrations © 2008, Axel Scheffler (2008, Scholastic Children's Books). Every effort has been made to trace copyright holders for the works reproduced in this book, and the publishers apologise for any inadvertent omissions.

Stick Man

About the book

Stick Man is a dark tale of the dangers that exist for a stick in the big wide world. The book tells the story of Stick Man, who lives happily in the family tree with his Stick Lady Love and their *stick children three*.

One day, tragedy strikes when Stick Man goes out for a jog and he is picked up and carried off by a dog. Stick Man tries his best to get home but is confronted with problems and dangers as he is repeatedly mistaken for an ordinary stick. He is put to good use in many ways but poor Stick Man just wants to get home. Stick Man ends up in a fire grate but his rescue ensures that he does not come to a 'sticky' end!

Stick Man encounters frustration, loneliness and loss as he is taken further and further away from his family and home. A repeating refrain (*I'm Stick Man*, I'm Stick Man, *I'M STICK MAN, that's me...*) shows that Stick Man is sure of his identity but it appears that other characters in the book are not so aware. This allows children to explore the nature of true identity and what is important to us in our lives.

At times, Stick Man is so weary that he is unaware of the dangers that lie ahead. The reader is taken on a journey of suspense, anxiety and, at last, relief, as a helpful friend ensures a happy ending.

The story is framed within the changing seasons, making this an ideal book to explore the natural world through cross-curricular and thematic work. It allows plenty of opportunities for enquiry and dialogue about living things, the fun and dangers of journeys, and the importance of family.

About the author

Julia Donaldson was born in 1948 and grew up in London. She is a singer, songwriter, performer, playwright and author. Her first jobs included teaching, publishing, busking and writing songs for children's television programmes. One of her first songs, *A Squash and a Squeeze*, was turned into a book, launching her career as an author in 1993. She has since written more than 150 books.

Julia studied at Bristol University where she met her husband, Malcolm, a paediatrician who often performs with her and accompanies her on guitar. Many of Julia's books are written in rhyme, combining her love of music and poetry.

About the illustrator

Axel Scheffler was born in 1957 in Germany. He grew up in Hamburg, and came to the UK to study illustration. After graduating in Bath, he moved to London, where he continues to live with his family. Axel has illustrated dozens of successful children's books. His many picture books include twelve written by Julia Donaldson. He has also created black-and-white line drawings for a wide range of older fiction.

Facts and figures

Julia Donaldson and Axel Scheffler have won many awards for their picture books, including the Smarties Prize and the Blue Peter Award for the Best Book to Read Aloud for *The Gruffalo*. Julia was teamed up with Axel Scheffler for their first publication *A Squash and a Squeeze,* and an award-winning team was created.

Guided reading

Introducing the book

Guided reading sessions will reinforce and develop the children's key reading skills. Help them to use phonological and grammatical knowledge to decode words. Encourage appropriate pace and emphasis on rhyme. Invite children to predict key moments and ask questions to develop their understanding of the text.

As well as exploring the story in readable chunks, it is essential that the children have opportunities to listen to and enjoy it without interruption. This will allow them to appreciate the sing-song rhythm and humour of the story and revel in the expressive illustrations.

Cover and title page

Display the cover and invite the children to describe what they see. Draw attention to the title, which is designed in a stick font. Point out that the title is framed within the trees with Stick Man below.

Encourage the children to make judgements about Stick Man. Ask questions such as: *Is he happy, mischievous or scared? Does the cover hint at any problems Stick Man may encounter?* Invite the children to offer predictions about the story content from the cover or title.

Now look at the title page. Again, both the font and the characters embed the idea that this story brings sticks to life. Ask the children: *What does this picture tell us about Stick Man? What do we think about Stick Man now we see him with his family?*

Who is Stick Man?

Read the first two sentences together. Point out the play on words of *the family tree*. Ask the children: *What is a family tree?*

The characters are known only as Stick Man, Stick Lady Love and stick children. Invite the children to suggest suitable names for the characters that begin with a 'st' blend.

Continue to read the text. What do the children notice about the font of the last line? Why do

they think it might be written in italics? (This could indicate that we, as readers, are warning Stick Man of the danger ahead.)

Danger!

Turn to the next spread. Read the text and look at the pictures. Talk about other tricks a dog could do without needing a stick. Work together with the children to come up with a phrase about any of these tricks following a similar format to *I'll fetch it and drop it*.

Look closely at the illustration on the right-hand page of the spread. Point out how much movement is conveyed in the detail. Ask the children for examples of words that describe the ways in which the people, animals and objects are moving.

Into the river

Turn to the next spread, about Pooh-sticks. Look at the first page, pointing out the different spellings of the 'ea/ee' digraph in *lead* and *freed*.

Ask the children to identify which sentence conveys Stick Man's happiness at being freed (*with a hop and a twirl*). What other expressions can they think of that are similar to this phrase (for example *hop and skip*; *hop and a jump*; *hop, skip and jump*)?

Find out if the children have ever played Pooh-sticks. Ask: *Could the girl use anything else instead of a stick?*

A swan's life

Turn to the page beginning *"I'm not a Pooh-stick!"* Look at the different ways in which the words *I'm Stick Man* are presented in Stick Man's repeated refrain. Ask the children: *What effect do the different font styles have on the way the reader reads the phrase?*

Notice how the story on the left-hand page is about Stick Man and the right-hand page about the swan.

On the next page, look at the three swan illustrations and read the text. Ask: *Do the*

Guided reading

illustrations match what is being said in the text? Invite the children to describe what is happening in the series of pictures (which show the story from the swans' viewpoint).

A beach holiday

Turn to the next page, which begins *He tosses and turns*. Read the text and ask the children to point out any alliteration they can see in the text (*tosses and turns*; *frolicking foam*). Can they think of alliterative adjectives to describe the following words: *waves, beach, dad*?

Challenge the children to work out how Stick Man might escape from the top of the sandcastle.

What am I?

On the following spread, read the text on the left-hand page and cover up the words on the right-hand page. Write four labels: *pen, bow, bat* and *boomerang*. Persuade the children to read the labels and match them to the illustrations. Then uncover the text and read it together.

Look carefully at these four pictures and ask the children what they observe about the passage of time. How long do they think Stick Man has been away from home? (Earlier pictures will give the children clues.)

In the snow

Turn to the next spread, with the snowman illustrations. Compare the illustration on the left-hand page with the one on the next spread. Invite the children to play 'Spot the difference' with the two illustrations. Ask questions such as: *What time of day is it? How can you tell? Which animals can you see? How does snow make you feel? Does everybody think snow is fun? Who doesn't and why not?*

On the page beginning *Stick Man is lonely*, read the text together. Point out the author's use of language. Here she uses the word *lonely* with *lost*. Can the children find another example of alliteration on this page (*frozen* and *frost*)?

Read the last line from this page again. Point out the dots at the end of the text. Ask: *Is this the end of the sentence? Why are the dots there?* Explain that the purpose of a cliffhanger is to create an atmosphere of suspense. Encourage the children to predict what might happen next. Challenge them to make their ideas as dramatic as possible.

The end of Stick Man?

Continue to the spread commencing *Or the voice saying* and read the text together. Tell the children that the story has reached its dramatic climax. Ask the children what emotions they feel at this point.

Read this spread again and, this time, ask the children to read using expression, thinking about the emotions they described. Ask: *Why is the reader more worried at this point than Stick Man?*

Stuck up the chimney

Before reading the text on the next spread, ask the children to read the pictures. What do they think is happening? Encourage them to use dramatic language. Make a list of words that could be used to heighten suspense to describe what Stick Man dreams, feels, hears and does. (For example: *rumble, tremble, shake, crash*.)

Now read the text together. Did the children use any of the actual words in their own descriptions? (For example: *shout, wiggle, shove*.)

A sooty landing

Turn to the spread beginning *And Santa falls into the room with a thump!* Look at the way the first sentence is presented. Why is the text larger? (This shows the reader that something dramatic has happened and quite loudly too!)

Have the children noticed what time the clock reads? Ask: *What is special about midnight? Can you think of any other stories that use midnight as a magical hour?*

Point out the use of exclamation marks and talk about how they instruct the reader to use expression in their voices.

Guided reading

Boys and girls

Read the text together on the following spread. Ask the children to list some of the presents the girl and the boy might have in their stockings. Ask questions such as: *Why do boys and girls have different toys? What identifies whether a toy is for a girl or a boy? Does it matter what children like to play with? What toys could Santa bring that are suitable for both boys and girls?*

Back in the family tree…

Turn to the page commencing *Stick Lady's lonely.* Read the text together and ask the children to think about which words describe an emotion (*sad, lonely*) and which imply emotion (*toss, turn*).

Can they imagine what the stick children might think is on the roof? Ask: *Would a bird, bat or mouse 'clatter'?* Give each child a pre-prepared label and ask them to decode the word and match it to one of these animals. (Labels could read: *scuttling, flapping, scratching, clawing, fluttering, squawking, screeching, squeaking* and so on.)

Challenge the children to predict what will happen next.

A happy ending

On the last spread, notice how the illustration portrays the ending of the story. Did the children predict that Santa was going to take Stick Man home?

Ask: *How do you think the family feels now? What other words could be used to describe happiness? Can all presents be gift wrapped?* Ask the children to think about what would be their best Christmas surprise ever.

End page and back cover

Look together at the end page and discuss how Stick Man is enjoying time with his family again. Encourage the children to recall some of his adventures. Persuade them to describe these adventures in the first person as if they were Stick Man talking to his children. Open the book carefully and notice how the cover illustration continues across the front and back covers. Ask the children to describe what is happening in the illustration.

Now read the blurb on the back cover. Does this text tell us anything about the plot? What additional information could be added that does not give away too much of the story?

Shared reading

Extract 1

● Read an enlarged copy of the text together.
● Conceal the extract from the children's view and draw a blank notice on the board. Ask a volunteer to see if they can remember what was written on the notice in the extract and write it down.
● Write another notice that might be found in a park. (*Keep off the grass, No ball games.*) Challenge the children to work out phonetically what your notice says.
● Ask the children: *What is different about the*

text written on the notice in the extract? Why is it written in capital letters? Ask the children to suggest other places they may see capital letters used and why.
● Invite the children to highlight words in the text that suggest an action or movement (*freed, sets off, hop, twirl, winning*). Explain that these words are verbs. Can they think of any other examples of verbs for movements or actions shown in the illustrations? Make a list of them (*kneel, stand, point, run* and so on).

Extract 2

● Look together at the illustration from the first spread of this extract, without reading the text. Ask: *What does the picture show? Are the characters in the illustration happy? Which words could you use to describe how they feel?*
● Now read the enlarged text together and ask the children to think about the emotions conveyed by this text. Do the words match their ideas about the illustrations?
● Ask volunteers to highlight words that show

how Stick Man is feeling (*lonely, lost, frozen, weary*). Can the children think of any other words to describe Stick Man's feelings?
● Look at the illustrations from the next spread of this extract and, again, think about the contrast between the text and the illustration.
● Ask the children to underline the last sentence and read it with expression. Discuss why this sentence is so important to the story and its role as a dramatic tool.

Extract 3

● Read the enlarged text together and ask the children to think about the rhyming words.
● Ask the children to find all the rhyming words in the text and look at the spelling of these words. Ask: *Which words do not have the same written endings?* (*Bed* and *head*.)
● Challenge the children to think of as many words as they can that rhyme with *bed* (*said, bread, red* and so on) and generate a list. Ask: *Do all the words end in 'ed'?* Which other

digraph spellings can the children see in these rhyming words?
● Now ask the children to circle all the words that contain the digraph 'ou' (*mouse, house, sound* and *could*). Ask: *Which word is the odd one out and why?* (*Could* has a different pronunciation.) Are there any other words that rhyme with 'could' that are spelled with an 'ou' (*would* and *should*)?
● Which words would the children use to sum up the mood of this extract?

Extract 1

A notice says:

DOGS MUST BE KEPT ON THE LEAD.

At last the game's over, and Stick Man is freed.

He sets off for home with a hop and a twirl.

Stick Man, oh Stick Man, beware of the girl!

"A stick!" cries the girl
    with a smile on her face.

"The right kind of Pooh-stick
    for winning the race!

Text © 2008, Julia Donaldson; Illustration © 2008, Axel Scheffler.

Extract 2

Stick Man is lonely, Stick Man is lost.

Stick Man is frozen and covered in frost.

Stick Man is weary. His eyes start to close.

He stretches and yawns and lies down for a doze.

He can't hear the bells, or the sweet-singing choir...

Or the voice saying, "Here's a good stick for the fire!"

Stick Man is lying asleep in the grate.

Can anyone wake him before it's too late?

Text © 2008, Julia Donaldson; Illustration © 2008, Axel Scheffler.

Extract 3

Stick Lady's lonely. The children are sad.

It won't feel like Christmas without their Stick Dad.

They toss and they turn in the family bed.

But what is that clattering sound overhead?

Someone is tumbling into their house.

Is it a bird, or a bat, or a mouse?

Or could it...yes, could it just possibly be...

Plot, character and setting

The family tree

Objective: To visualise and comment on characters and ideas, making imaginative links to their own experiences.
What you need: One enlarged copy of photocopiable page 15 and one copy for each child.
Cross-curricular link: History.

What to do

● Display the enlarged copy of photocopiable page 15. Read the story and ask the children to tell you what they know about the Stick family.
● Encourage the children to tell you about their own relatives. (For example: aunts, cousins, uncles and grandparents.) Make a list of these titles. How many different titles are grandparents known by in your class?
● Explain that each leaf represents a person in Stick Man's family tree. The lower branches represent the youngest family members and the higher ones represent the oldest. Using the enlarged copy of page 15, invite a volunteer to draw a stick figure on one of the bottom branch leaves to represent one of the stick children. Now ask where they should draw Stick Man. Ask: *Why does this branch have two joined leaves?* (This is to show that Stick Man has married Stick Lady Love.) Who do the children think could be drawn in one of the top branch leaves? Where would they put Stick Man's brother?
● Finally, ask the children to fill in their individual Stick Man family trees, using the correct titles from the stick children's viewpoint.

Differentiation
For older/more confident learners: Challenge the children to research their own family trees (be sensitive to individual situations).
For younger/less confident learners: Provide word labels to help children record their answers.

Changing seasons

Objective: To consider how mood and atmosphere are created in live or recorded performance.
What you need: Music – *The Four Seasons* by Vivaldi, four large sheets of paper, pens and a large space to move around in.
Cross-curricular links: Dance, music.

What to do

● Look through the book together and ask the children to identify parts of the story that take place in winter, spring, summer and autumn. Make a list of significant events that happen to Stick Man under these four headings. Challenge the children to find pictorial clues that show the changing seasons. (For example: the weather, the clothes that people are wearing and the activities that are taking place.)
● Listen together to the music by Vivaldi and invite the children to comment on how the music represents each season. Divide the class into four and ask each group to work on one of the seasons. Ask them to make a mind map using the following thinking points: weather, clothes, feelings, things to do and places to go.
● Play the music quietly in the background while the children have thinking, talking and writing time. Explain that they will use their mind maps as a basis for a piece of dance/movement.
● In a large space, allow time for each group to rehearse movements based on their ideas. Play the music again and persuade each group to share their performance.

Differentiation
For older/more confident learners: Use a video recorder and ask children to analyse their performance, commenting on what elements worked well and what they could improve upon.
For younger/less confident learners: Model a variety of suggested movements and actions for the children to practise.

Plot, character and setting

Flotsam and jetsam

Objective: To enjoy listening to and using spoken and written language and readily turn to it in play and learning.
What you need: A copy of *Stick Man*, a water tray or trays, a selection of natural and man-made objects for floating and sinking experiments including the items on photocopiable page 16, a copy of photocopiable page 16 for each child, pens.
Cross-curricular link: Science.

What to do

● Revisit the seaside spread in *Stick Man,* which begins *He tosses and turns.* Ask the children to comment on what they can see at the edge of the shore. Ask: *Where have these things come from? What else might the tide bring in?*
● Explain the phrase 'flotsam and jetsam' (ships' goods that are lost at sea). How do the children think things are lost at sea? (The items might have been lost in a shipwreck, or thrown or dropped overboard.) The expression is more commonly used now to mean odds and ends, bits and pieces.
● Send small groups of children to the water tray(s). Invite the children to discover which items from the collection would be classed as 'flotsam and jetsam', that is, things that would float on the water and be washed ashore, and which would be 'lagan', which is the word for goods or wreckage that lie at the bottom of the sea.
● Ask the children to record their findings on photocopiable page 16.

Differentiation
For older/more confident learners: Challenge children to find out more about shipwrecks and the definitions of flotsam and jetsam.
For younger/less confident learners: Encourage children to record their findings pictorially.

Stick Man actions

Objective: To create short simple texts on paper that combine words with images.
What you need: A copy of *Stick Man*, a whiteboard or large paper, copies of photocopiable page 17 for each child.
Cross-curricular links: Art and design, drama.

What to do

● Read through the story and ask the children to think about any language in the text that describes a movement or action. (For example: *He sets off home with a hop and a twirl; Get ready to throw!; He drifts down the river.*) They should comment on whether these actions are made by Stick Man or done to him.
● Ask for volunteers to draw a simple representation of Stick Man performing the movement for one of the verbs on the whiteboard. Invite others to demonstrate with their bodies what this action or movement looks like in a still pose.
● Encourage volunteers to create their own action poses. Challenge the rest of the group to guess the verbs being acted out.
● Hand out copies of photocopiable page 17 and ask the children to read the words and draw their own simple stick men pictures to illustrate the words.

Differentiation
For older/more confident learners: Children could make flick books showing a movement such as flying or jumping.
For younger/less confident learners: Provide support to read the labels on the photocopiable sheet.

Plot, character and setting

Help Stick Man to get home

> **Objective:** To use talk to organise, sequence and clarify thinking, ideas, feelings and events.
> **What you need:** A copy of *Stick Man*, pens, large sheets of paper.
> **Cross-curricular links:** Science, geography.

What to do
● Re-read the story and ask the children to highlight parts of the story where Stick Man travels. Ask the children: *In what ways does he journey away from and back to his family tree?* (He runs, floats down the river and across the sea, is carried by a dog and children, thrown as a boomerang and given a lift on a sleigh.)
● Invite the children to design a pictorial map working in small groups. Each group should decide how Stick Man could get home from the fireplace to his family tree. The challenge is to find five different ways of getting home, including at least one method of crossing the ocean. On their maps they must also include: a dangerous swamp, a high mountain, a waterfall and a wide, fast flowing river. They may choose to include other obstacles to hinder Stick Man's journey.
● Ask: *What transport or inventions could be used to help Stick Man?* The children should negotiate, draw and write brief descriptions on their map, adding as much information as necessary.

> **Differentiation**
> **For older/more confident learners:** Challenge children to write up Stick Man's imaginary journey as a piece of diary writing.
> **For younger/less confident learners:** Allow opportunities to develop role play based on difficult journeys.

I'm Stick Man, I'm Stick Man!

> **Objective:** To listen with enjoyment and respond to stories, songs, rhymes and poems and to make up their own stories, songs, rhymes and poems.
> **What you need:** A collection of wooden claves or rhythm sticks, a copy of *Stick Man*, a large sheet of paper or whiteboard.
> **Cross-curricular link:** Music.

What to do
● Re-read the story together and ask the children to join in with all the refrains of *I'm Stick Man, I'm Stick Man, I'M STICK MAN, that's me,* plus the following sentence ending with the words *family tree.*
● Invite the children to clap out the beat of the refrain. Ask them: *How many beats are in this two sentence refrain?* (There are eight beats.) Ask the children to identify which words the beat falls on. It might help to write the refrain on the board and ask the children to underline these words. (In the first place this occurs, the beat falls three times on *stick*, then on *me, want, home,* the first syllable of *family* and finally *tree.*)
● Allow time for the children to practise tapping out this beat with their sticks.
● Now ask the children if they can identify the rhythm. This time, point out that the children are tapping out the spoken syllables. Again, illustrate this by highlighting the syllables on the board.
● Challenge the children to invent their own rhymes that follow the same beat and rhythm.

> **Differentiation**
> **For older/more confident learners:** Encourage children to compose a whole song based on this refrain.
> **For younger/less confident learners:** Work together to compose the new rhymes and perform together.

Plot, character and setting

Home, sweet home

> **Objective:** To use language to imagine and recreate roles and experiences.
> **What you need:** A copy of *Stick Man*; shoe boxes or similar; a collection of natural objects and recycled materials such as match boxes, matchsticks with tips cut off, lolly sticks, cotton reels, bottle tops, moss, bark and twigs; glue, scissors and paints.
> **Cross-curricular links:** Art and design, design and technology, geography.

What to do

● Look together at the last two spreads of the book, showing the interior of the family tree. Ask the children to explain what items they can see and what they are made from. Ask questions such as: *What did the stick children three use to draw on the walls? How do they keep warm? What do they sit on? What might the stick children like to play with? What are their toys made from?*

● Ask the children to compare the interior of the tree with their own homes. What do they have that the stick people do not and why? Explain that the stick people can only use natural or recycled materials.

● Challenge the children to work individually or in pairs to create their own homes for the stick family using only the materials provided. Encourage the children to make the finished homes look as much like rooms in a tree as possible.

> **Differentiation**
> **For older/more confident learners:** Ask children to write a brief explanation of how they designed their family tree.
> **For younger/less confident learners:** Provide support by modelling possible uses for objects, for example: *I wonder what this could be. What shape is it?*

Which present?

> **Objective:** To use talk to organise, sequence and clarify thinking, ideas, feelings and events.
> **What you need:** An enlarged copy of photocopiable page 18 cut into six cards (three pairs), a copy of *Stick Man*.
> **Cross-curricular links:** PSHE/philosophy.

What to do

● Look at the illustration on the final spread where Stick Man is reunited with his family. Ask the children: *What do you think could be inside the stick children's presents? Do you think the stick children would rather have their presents or their father?*

● Place the first pair of cards from photocopiable page 18 on the floor, spread well apart. Explain that the children must think about which present

they would rather have. Ask them to stand next to the card that represents their choice.

● Encourage the children to talk to classmates standing by the same card about their reasons for choosing that present. Ask for volunteers to share some of these ideas with the whole class.

● Repeat with the other cards, ensuring children are able to justify their choices with a valid reason and follow on from the ideas of others.

> **Differentiation**
> **For older/more confident learners:** Encourage children to facilitate by asking questions to promote deeper thinking, for example, *What if...* or *Would that always be a better option?*
> **For younger/less confident learners:** Ensure less confident speakers are given support to share their ideas within the safety of a small group.

Family tree

● Pretend you are one of the stick children. Complete the stick family tree by writing names in the leaves.

Illustrations © 2010, Anna Godwin/Beehive Illustration.

Flotsam and jetsam

● Put the following objects, and any others that your teacher has given you, into the water one by one. Add the items to the table to show if they are 'flotsam and jetsam' (they float) or 'lagan' (they sink).

Flotsam and jetsam	Lagan

READ & RESPOND: Activities based on Stick Man

Illustrations © 2010, Anna Godwin/Beehive Illustration.

Stick Man actions

● Draw your own simple stick man pictures to show the meaning of the action words.

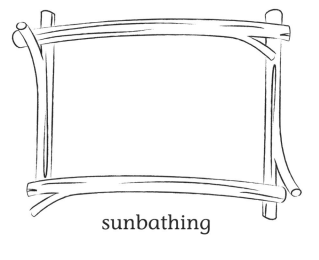

sunbathing

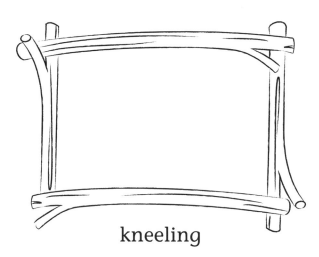

kneeling

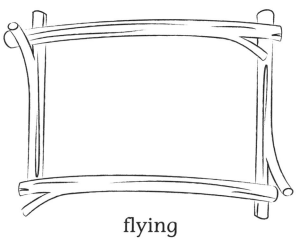

flying

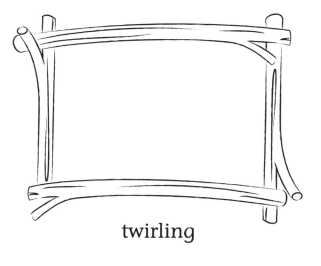

twirling

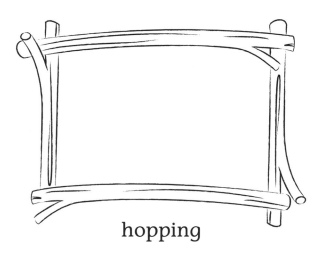

hopping

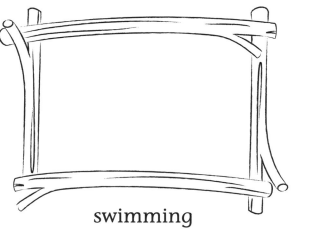

swimming

Illustrations © 2010, Anna Godwin/Beehive Illustration.

Plot, character and setting

Which present?

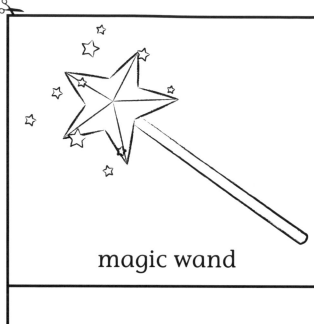

magic wand

box of treasure

television

flying carpet

scary costume

clown costume

Illustrations © 2010, Anna Godwin/Beehive Illustration.

Talk about it

Winter or summer?

Objective: To use talk to organise, sequence and clarify thinking, ideas, feelings and events.
What you need: Two scenario cards (with illustrations for younger children) labelled: *It should be winter all year round* and *It should be summer all year round*.
Cross-curricular links: Geography, science, PSHE.

What to do

● Look through *Stick Man* as a class to remind the children which seasons feature heavily in the story. Note how the cold winter days leave Stick Man feeling sad and weary.
● Ask the children to imagine that there were no seasons and that the weather remained the same all year round. Which season would the children prefer?
● Divide the class into two groups and give each group one of the scenario cards. Explain that each group should discuss together all the positive and negative things about their statements.
● Ask the groups to consider the impact of the summer or winter weather on all the following things: the environment, animals and the natural world, fun and celebrations, people of all ages.
● Bring the two groups back together to share ideas. Encourage the children to listen carefully to the benefits and problems presented.
● Allow the children to vote on which scenario they would prefer by standing next to the appropriate card. Which one has the majority vote?

Differentiation
For older/more confident learners: Encourage children to take notes of the group's dialogue.
For younger/less confident learners: Allow children to gain confidence in smaller groups or to discuss their ideas with a partner.

Alive or not alive?

Objective: To take turns to speak and listen to each other's suggestions.
What you need: An enlarged copy of photocopiable page 22 cut into six cards, two large sheets of paper headed *Alive* and *Not alive*.
Cross-curricular links: Science, PSHE/philosophy.

What to do

● Ask the children to sit in an 'enquiry circle'. Remind them that they must speak respectfully and listen carefully to each other's ideas and questions.
● Prompt the children to think about what Stick Man was made out of. Ask: *Why was Stick Man alive?* Spread the six cards out in the middle of the circle. Ask for volunteers to choose a card and place it under one of the headings *Alive* or *Not alive*.
● Encourage the children to share their ideas with the group about which objects they think are alive and which are not alive, and to justify their reasons. Encourage other children to push for deeper thinking by using language of discussion such as: *What makes you think that? What evidence do you have to back up your statement? I agree/disagree because... Have you considered...*
● The following questions may be useful for your discussion: *What makes something alive? What is the difference between alive and living? What makes Stick Man different from other sticks? Can something be alive in our minds?*

Differentiation
For older/more confident learners: Encourage children to look for and identify inconsistent thinking and press for deeper thinking.
For younger/less confident learners: Present ideas as statements and ask children to use double-sided voting cards to indicate whether they agree or disagree with the statement.

Talk about it

What am I?

Objective: To explore familiar themes through improvisation and role play.
What you need: Several sticks of different lengths and sizes.
Cross-curricular link: Drama.

What to do

● Look through the book together and talk about all the things that Stick Man was used for (a dog's game of 'fetch', a Pooh-stick, a swan's nest, a mast for a flag, a sword, a hook for a bag, a pen, a bow, a bat, a boomerang, an arm for a snowman and firewood).
● Explain that the children are going to work together in groups to find as many uses for the stick as possible.
● Pick up a stick and demonstrate one or two possible uses. (For example: a cricket bat and a broom.) Ask the children to guess what your mime showed.
● Divide the class into small groups and ask each group to choose a stick to work with. Suggest that the children pass the stick around the group as they discuss their ideas about the different ways in which it could be used. Allow about five minutes' discussion time.
● Bring the class back together and ask volunteers from each group to perform their actions and challenge the other groups to guess what the stick is.
● Discuss together whether the size or shape of stick changed how they could use it.

Differentiation
For older/more confident learners: Challenge the children to list as many things as they can that are made from wood.
For younger/less confident learners: Provide clues for things they could use the stick for.

Odd one out

Objective: To speak clearly and audibly with confidence and control, and show awareness of the listener.
What you need: An enlarged copy of photocopiable page 23 cut into cards.
Cross-curricular link: Drama.

What to do

● Look at the illustrations on the page beginning *I'm not a pen!* Ask the children to find the odd one out from the choice of *pen, bow, bat* and *boomerang.*
● Ensure any ideas are backed up with a valid justification. (For example: *Pen, because it starts with 'p' and the others start with 'b'.* Or: *Pen, because the others all involve some kind of physical activity.*)
● Explain that by choosing an odd one out, the children had to look for similarities and differences between the objects. Display the cards from photocopiable page 23 and allow the children some silent time to think about how the objects are used, their appearance, or any other features they possess.
● Invite a volunteer to choose a selection of three cards, including one card that is different in some way from the other two. Ask the volunteer to display the cards on the board.
● Can the rest of the class guess which card is the odd one out and why? You may discover some ideas that the original volunteer had not thought of.

Differentiation
For older/more confident learners: Encourage children to make their own lists of objects to use in this activity.
For younger/less confident learners: Allow additional opportunities for thinking and talking about similarities and differences between objects and pictures.

Talk about it

Tree guessing game

> **Objective:** To listen to others in class, ask relevant questions and follow instructions.
> **What you need:** Copies of photocopiable page 24 (one per pair).
> **Cross-curricular link:** Science.

What to do

● Ask the children to help compile a list of things that they might associate with a tree. (For example: leaves, fruit, nuts, moss, insects, ivy, nests, squirrels, birds, roots, owls and so on.)

● Request a volunteer to come to the front and secretly choose something from the list. Write the numerals 1 to 15 on the board and explain that the rest of the group may ask 15 questions to try to guess the mystery object. The volunteer may only answer yes or no and should mark off a number each time a question is asked.

● Ask for, or suggest, some questions such as:

Has it got legs? Has it got feathers? Does it fall off the tree? Is it edible? What colour is it? Could it live without the tree? Could the tree live without it?

● Hand out copies of photocopiable page 24, one between two. One child in each pair should secretly draw something on one side of the tree. The paper should then be folded over so that the drawing is covered but one set of numerals can be seen and marked off. The other partner has to ask yes/no questions to find out what has been drawn. The partners then swap roles, folding the paper the other way. The winner is the person who revealed the object using the fewest questions.

> **Differentiation**
> **For older/more confident learners:** Challenge children to research trees further.
> **For younger/less confident learners:** Provide support in the form of clues and by formatting questions to ask.

Stick Man dreams

> **Objective:** To use talk to organise, sequence and clarify thinking, ideas, feelings and events.
> **What you need:** A copy of *Stick Man*.
> **Cross-curricular links:** PSHE/philosophy.

What to do

● Look together at the spread where Stick Man is asleep in the grate. Ask: *What might Stick Man be dreaming about?*

● Form a circle and ask the children if any of them would like to share any of their dreams with the group. Have the children had any dreams which are similar? Is it because of shared experiences or anxieties?

● Ask the following philosophical questions and remind the children to listen to each other's ideas respectfully, to show courteous listening and to work together to see if they can reach any agreements about their ideas: *What is a dream? How can we see dreams if our eyes are shut?*

Where do dreams come from? Can you have dreams if you are awake? Can dreams really come true? Can you dream of something you have never experienced? Is there a difference between dreaming and imagining? How do we know we are not dreaming right now?

● Encourage the use of language of enquiry and discussion. (For example: *I agree/disagree because… Can you give me an example of that? How do we know that is true? The other side of that argument might be…*)

> **Differentiation**
> **For older/more confident learners:** Allow children to take more of a facilitator's role by encouraging them to invite others into the dialogue and ask questions to push for further reasoning.
> **For younger/less confident learners:** Allow time for less confident speakers to gain confidence by listening or allowing time for speaking in small groups or partners first.

Alive or not alive?

READ & RESPOND: Activities based on *Stick Man*

SCHOLASTIC
www.scholastic.co.uk

Illustration © 2008, Axel Scheffler. Illustrations © 2010, Anna Godwin/Beehive Illustration.

Talk about it

Odd one out

Tree guessing game

- Draw a picture on one side of the tree.
- Fold the paper over so your drawing is hidden.
- Your partner will ask up to 15 questions to guess what you have drawn. Cross off a number after each question is asked.

Player 1
1
2
3
4
5
6
7
8
9
10
11
12
13
14
15

Player 2
1
2
3
4
5
6
7
8
9
10
11
12
13
14
15

Illustration © 2010, Anna Godwin/Beehive Illustration.

READ & RESPOND: Activities based on *Stick Man*

Get writing

Message in a bottle

> **Objective:** To use key features of narrative in their own independent writing.
> **What you need:** A copy of *Stick Man*, a copy of photocopiable page 28 for each child, a globe.
> **Cross-curricular link:** Geography.

What to do

● Look together at the spread beginning *He tosses and turns, till the frolicking foam*. Read the first block of text which tells how Stick Man gets washed up on a beach far from home. Ask the children: *Is it possible that Stick Man is now in a different country?* Look together at the globe and show how Great Britain is an island surrounded by water. Ask: *Which countries could Stick Man have ended up in?*
● Look again at the illustration and challenge the children to find something that Stick Man could use to send a message home. (There is a bottle by the rocks.)
● Explain that the children are going to write a message from Stick Man to put in the bottle. Give each child a copy of photocopiable page 28 and ask them to compose Stick Man's message, reminding them to write in the first person. The message should explain how they know they are in a different country and which country they think they have landed in. Is there anything else Stick Man might want to tell his family?

> **Differentiation**
> **For older/more confident learners:** Challenge the children to write about the shortest and longest journeys across the sea from Great Britain.
> **For younger/less confident learners:** Provide key words taken from the class discussion to use as prompts.

How to play Pooh-sticks

> **Objectives:** To write simple instructions; to write chronological texts using simple structures.
> **What you need:** A copy of *Stick Man*; access to a computer/whiteboard set up with the following webpage: www.just-pooh.com/poohsticks.html
> **Cross-curricular links:** Geography, history.

What to do

● Look together at the spread beginning *A notice says: DOGS MUST BE KEPT ON THE LEAD*. Read the text that is relevant to Pooh-sticks. Ask the children if they have ever played Pooh-sticks. Do they know why it is called Pooh-sticks? Explain that this game was 'invented' by Pooh Bear and look together at the following web page: www.just-pooh.com/poohsticks.html
● Read the instructions and talk about how the game works (the river carries a floating object downstream towards the sea and under a bridge). Ask: *What else could you use to play this game?*
● Explain to the children that you would like them to write their own set of instructions for the game of Pooh-sticks using the correct chronological sequence of steps. Discuss what might happen if the instructions are written out of sequence.

> **Differentiation**
> **For older/more confident learners:** Allow time for additional research into the history and geography of Pooh-sticks and Pooh bridge in Ashdown Forest using the following webpage: www.just-pooh.com/ashdown.html
> **For younger/less confident learners:** Provide picture clues in order to write simple instructions.

Get writing

Swans

Objective: To show an understanding of how information can be found in non-fiction texts to answer questions about where, who, why and how.
What you need: A copy of *Stick Man*, copies of non-fiction books about swans, access to the internet.
Cross-curricular link: Science.

What to do

● Look together at *Stick Man* and ask the children to find the pages that depict Stick Man's stay with the swans. Encourage the children to talk about what they know about swans. Ask: *What words could we use to describe the swans? What do the illustrations tell us about them?*

● Ask the children to work with partners or in small groups to research swans then to write a short information booklet for Stick Man. Discuss what types of information might be useful to Stick Man in his situation. For example: *Are swans dangerous? If so, when and why? How long can Stick Man expect to stay on the swan's nest from the time the eggs are laid until the time they hatch? How many eggs will there be? Who will look after the eggs? What else is special about swans?* (They are a protected species. Why?)

● Allow time for the children to share their written facts with the class.

Differentiation
For older/more confident learners: Encourage children to use detailed descriptive language and present their work in the style of a pamphlet.
For younger/less confident learners: Allow children to draw their information and scribe or model their written explanations of research.

Pooh-stick spelling

Objective: To spell new words using phonics as the prime approach.
What you need: An enlarged copy of photocopiable page 29 and individual copies for each child.

What to do

● Explain that the children are going to play a game based on the classic game of Pooh-sticks. The idea of the game is to collect pine cones that contain phonemes and Pooh-sticks that contain digraphs to make as many words as they can.

● Demonstrate one or two examples using the enlarged copy. Words can range from simple CVC constructions using pine cones only, for example *man*, to compound words using a combination of pine cones and Pooh-sticks, for example *teaspoon*.

● Give the children time to come up with as many words as they can in pairs or small groups, then collect examples from all the children. You may wish to provide children with letter tiles or cards that they can physically move around to spell and create new words.

● Ask the children to arrange their words into categories of two-letter words, three-letter words, four-letter words and more than four-letter words. Which is the longest word found? Which letters or digraphs have been most commonly used?

● Did the children use any methods to find their words? (For example: rhyming words, common word families and so on.)

Differentiation
For older/more confident learners: Challenge children to find words of four or more letters.
For younger/less confident learners: Start with simple CVC words using pine cones only.

Get writing

Missing poster

> **Objective:** To convey information and ideas in simple non-narrative forms.
> **What you need:** A copy of *Stick Man*, copies of photocopiable page 30.

What to do

● Re-read the story and ask the children to focus on the points of view of Stick Lady Love and the stick children. How do they think these characters felt when they realised that someone they loved had gone missing? (For example: Anxious? Worried? Heartbroken?) *What action might they take to find Stick Man? Would they call the police? What would their response be? Would they form a search party? Who might join the search and why?*

● Ask the children if they have ever had a cat or dog go missing or seen posters about missing animals. What information would a missing poster have to tell the reader?

● Compile a list of information that the children think would be needed in a 'Missing' poster for Stick Man. For example: name, description of appearance (height, weight, eye colour, hair colour, what he was wearing), things Stick Man likes to do, whether a reward is offered, why his family wants to find him, what someone should do if they see him.

● Give the children time to create their poster using photocopiable page 30. Encourage them to label their illustration using descriptive language.

> **Differentiation**
> **For older/more confident learners:** Ask children to write an additional letter in the form of a police 'missing person report'.
> **For younger/less confident learners:** Provide a word bank or scribe verbal ideas.

Stick Man writing

> **Objective:** To hear and say sounds in words in the order in which they occur.
> **What you need:** A large number of small twigs, matchsticks with tips cut off or lollipop sticks (enough for at least 20 per child plus extras for the artwork), a piece of A4 card for each child, glue.
> **Cross-curricular link:** Art and design.

What to do

● Give out the sticks and explain to the children that you are going to read out words from the story of *Stick Man* for them to spell. Tell the children that they will need to listen very carefully. Their task is to arrange the sticks to spell out the letters represented by the sounds they hear, in the order that they occur.

● Give the children an example such as *dog* and demonstrate how to arrange the sticks, sounding out the phonemes as you go along. Repeat this exercise a few times.

● Next, ask the children to choose one of the words they have spelled to use in a piece of artwork. Their artwork should include the word rendered in sticks and perhaps an illustration of the object. Good examples from the book might be *dog, swan, sand, pen, bow, bat, fire, toys* and *tree.*

● The children could also add leaves to their words to give them a more stick-like appearance.

> **Differentiation**
> **For older/more confident learners:** Add more complex words that contain digraphs to the challenge such as girl, danger and snowman.
> **For younger/less confident learners:** Provide support for the children to work in a small group working out the sounds and creating the words together.

Message in a bottle

● Write Stick Man's message to his family in the bottle.

Illustration © 2010, Anna Godwin/Beehive Illustration.